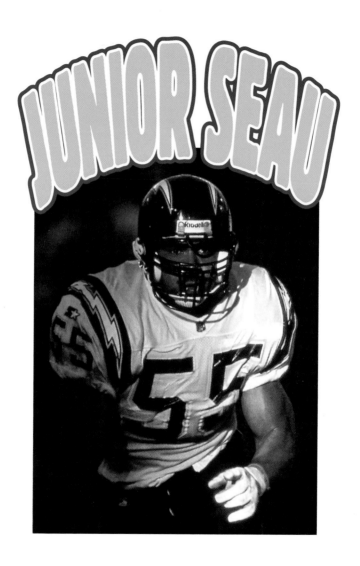

HIGH-VOLTAGE LINEBACKER
JUNIOR SEAU

Terri Morgan

Lerner Publications Company • Minneapolis

For Kelby

Information for this book was obtained from the following sources: 1995 USC Football Media Guide, The Associated Press, *Carlsbad Blade-Tribune*, *Cincinnati Enquirer*, Grolier's encyclopedia, interviews with Pat Kimbrel and Larry Smith, Junior Seau Foundation, *Los Angeles Times*, *New York Times*, San Diego Chargers 1995 Media Guide, *San Francisco Chronicle*, *San Jose Mercury News*, *Sport*, *The Sporting News*, and *Sports Illustrated*. The author gives special thanks to Laura Crosser.

This book is available in two editions:
Library binding by Lerner Publications Company
Soft cover by First Avenue Editions
241 First Avenue North, Minneapolis, Minnesota 55401

LIBRARY OF CONGRESS CATALOGING-IN-PUBLICATION DATA

Morgan, Terri.
Junior Seau : high voltage linebacker / Terri Morgan.
p.   cm.
Includes bibliographical references (p.   ).
Summary: Profiles the personal life and football career of the hard-working linebacker for the San Diego Chargers who helped his team get to Super Bowl XXIX.
ISBN 0-8225-2896-7 (hardcover : alk. paper). — ISBN 0-8225-9746-2 (pbk. : alk. paper)
1. Seau, Junior, 1969–   — Juvenile literature. 2. Football players — United States — Biography — Juvenile literature. 3. San Diego Chargers (Football team) — Juvenile literature. [1. Seau, Junior, 1969–
2. Football players. 3. Samoan Americans — Biography.] I. Title.
GV939.S393M67   1997
796.332'092—dc20
[B]   96-13113

Manufactured in the United States of America
1 2 3 4 5 6 – JR – 02 01 00 99 98 97

Contents

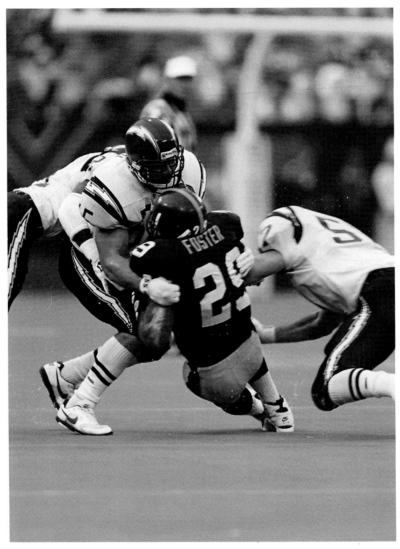

Junior brings down Pittsburgh running back Barry Foster in the American Football Conference (AFC) Championship Game.

Super Game

Junior Seau (SAY-ow) and his San Diego Charger teammates were steaming mad. The Chargers had advanced through the NFL playoffs and were in Pittsburgh preparing to face the Steelers for the 1994 AFC Championship. But the Steelers weren't taking the Chargers seriously. Pittsburgh's players were so confident about winning that they were already looking ahead to the Super Bowl.

The Chargers, who had won 11 games and lost 5 during the season, were the underdogs. Even though San Diego had defeated Pittsburgh in the final regular-season game, the Steelers dismissed the loss as a fluke. Since the team had already clinched its division, Steeler head coach Bill Cowher had used his second- and third-string players for most of the game. The Steelers bragged that they would have won the game if their starters had played more.

In radio, television, and newspaper interviews, Pittsburgh players boasted they would beat the Chargers. Steeler defensive end Ray Seals even promised that San Diego wouldn't score a single point. Several of his teammates, led by tight end Eric Green, spent part of the week recording a Super Bowl rap video.

The Steelers' arrogance angered Junior and his teammates. In front of reporters, the players kept quiet. In practice, however, the Chargers vented their feelings. San Diego head coach Bobby Ross called a team meeting to discuss Pittsburgh's lack of respect. He urged his players to prove themselves on the field.

"Nobody gives us any respect," Ross said. "No one has given us any respect all year long. You can't just talk a game, though. You have to go out and play."

No one on the San Diego team was more determined to do that than Junior Seau. The 6-foot-5, 255-pound defensive linebacker had been playing with a pinched nerve in his neck since late November. The injury was severe enough that Junior had difficulty lifting his left arm. Despite the pain, Junior's discipline and immense desire to play kept him from missing a single game. A football career can end at any time, he knew, so he was determined to make the most of every playing opportunity.

"I'm not guaranteed to step on the field ever again," Junior told a reporter for the Associated Press. "I'm given a Sunday, and what I do on that Sunday is what I'm judged on. And that's the way I approach things.

"You get the talent I was blessed with, and knowing that I have a window in my lifetime to go ahead and master it," Junior added, "I'm not going to let it pass without a fight."

Even though he played half the season in pain, the hardworking linebacker still managed to lead the Charger defense. He tackled 155 opponents during the regular season. By contrast, Darrien Gordon, the Chargers' second-leading tackler, had 89 tackles.

Physically overpowering, Junior is also mentally tough. He channeled his fury over the Steelers' boasting into the AFC Championship Game. Junior began unleashing his ire on his opponents as soon as he took the field.

On the first play after kickoff, Pittsburgh quarterback Neil O'Donnell handed off to running back Barry Foster. Junior sprang across the line of scrimmage, then darted to his left as the ball changed hands, and threw Foster to the ground. The running back staggered to his feet. Junior turned toward the Charger bench and pumped his healthy arm in exuberance.

"He was quiet before the game, just sitting in here and waiting," Charger safety Stanley Richard told *Sports Illustrated.* "And then, when the game started, he exploded."

A pumped-up Junior celebrates after getting a sack in the AFC Championship Game.

The explosion continued all afternoon. Led by Junior's 16 tackles, the Chargers stifled Pittsburgh's offense. They held the Steelers, who had rushed for an average 136.6 yards a game during the regular season, to 66 yards on the ground. Once Pittsburgh switched to its passing game, the Chargers began swarming around O'Donnell and his receivers.

With less than two minutes left in the game, Pittsburgh was closing in on the goal line and threatening the Chargers' 17-13 lead. Pittsburgh fullback John L. Williams was at the three-yard line when Junior stopped him with a punishing hit. Seconds later, linebacker Dennis Gibson batted away O'Donnell's fourth-down pass to Foster in the end zone. The Chargers won! San Diego was headed to the Super Bowl for the first time in franchise history!

In the locker room, Junior was quiet and serious while his teammates celebrated the big win. "You can never measure character," he said. "You can never measure heart. [But] you saw it out there today. This is a great moment for San Diego and for everyone in the organization."

Junior's parents, Tiaina Sr. and Luisa, join their famous son during a Charger rally to celebrate San Diego's AFC Championship.

2

A Samoan Family in America

Junior Seau was born in San Diego, California, on January 19, 1969, the fifth child of Tiaina and Luisa Seau. He was named Tiaina, after his father, but the family called him Junior to avoid confusing him with Tiaina Sr. Junior's parents were born and raised in American Samoa, where they met and married.

American Samoa is located in the South Pacific Ocean, about 1,600 miles northeast of New Zealand. It is a United States territory that consists of a chain of seven tropical islands. The island where Tiaina and Luisa lived is known as Aunuu.

About 45,000 people live on the islands of American Samoa, where Samoan and English are the most common languages. Most residents are of Polynesian descent, and many live in communal villages. While elected officials govern the islands, villagers rely on the wisdom of their chiefs to provide leadership.

Village chiefs are called *matais.* One of Junior Seau's great-grandfathers had been the matai of his village in Pago Pago, the capital of American Samoa.

Tiaina and Luisa moved their growing family to San Diego in 1964, about five years before Junior was born. When Junior was a baby, the Seau family moved back to their old village in American Samoa. They returned to California for good before Junior started kindergarten. The family settled in Oceanside, a small coastal city about 30 miles north of San Diego. The Seaus bought a small cottage in a poor neighborhood on the east side of Oceanside. Many other Samoan families lived nearby, including several of Junior's aunts, uncles, and cousins. A few years later, the Seaus' youngest child, Tony, was born, joining Junior, his older brothers David and Savaii, and sisters Mary and Annette.

Tiaina Sr. worked in a factory that manufactured rubber products. Later on, he began working as a custodian at a nearby school. Luisa took a job in a grocery store at the Camp Pendleton Marine Corps base and also worked in a laundromat.

The Seaus' home was in a rough part of town. Some of the neighbors belonged to gangs. Others abused drugs, vandalized the neighborhood with graffiti, or committed serious crimes. Tiaina and Luisa made sure Junior and his brothers and sisters stayed so busy they wouldn't be lured into trouble.

Religion was very important to the Seau family. Tiaina was a deacon in the First Samoan Congregational Church, where the family attended services on Sundays. At home, Tiaina led the family in prayers twice a day.

"Dad taught us about morals, values, and goals," Junior told *Sports Illustrated*. "Having a tight-knit family was important to him."

Samoan customs were also very important to Junior's father. While at home, the Seaus spoke only Samoan, and they wore traditional island clothing.

Two boys practice football on an island of American Samoa.

Junior's sisters dressed in long, colorful, loose-fitting dresses called *muumuus*. Junior and his brothers donned wraparound skirts called *lavalavas*. The boys practiced the Samoan slap dance, while their sisters danced the hula.

Junior's parents expected their children to work hard in school. At first school was difficult for Junior because he spoke only Samoan. It became easier for him as his English improved. By the time he finished elementary school, Junior could speak English as well as he could speak Samoan.

Tiaina was a loving but strict father. If the children misbehaved, they knew they would be punished. "There were a lot of spankings, with sticks, shoes, whatever was laying around," Junior's brother Savaii told *Sports Illustrated*. "If we even thought about going right after he told us to go to the left, we got our whippings."

Junior admired and respected his father, and he tried hard to please him. He acknowledges, however, that Tiaina could be intimidating. "My friends used to be so afraid of him that they'd stand in the middle of Zeiss Street and call for me to come out and play," Junior told *Sports Illustrated*.

The family's cottage had only two bedrooms. Luisa and Tiaina slept in one bedroom, and their two daughters slept in the other. Junior and his brothers spent their nights in the garage. The boys' bedroom had a cement floor, a leaky roof, and it housed the family's washing machine and household supplies.

"I had the right corner by the door," Junior said. "My two sisters, who lived inside the house, always bragged that they had a carpet in their bedroom. But we'd say, 'So what? We have the biggest door in the whole place.'"

The garage was chilly on winter nights, so Junior and his brothers used portable heaters to warm up their bedroom. Junior recalls those days fondly.

"We were never cold because the love was so warm," Junior told the *New York Times.* "We thought everyone slept in the garage. We didn't know any different."

Junior, David, and Savaii shared a love of sports and a love of Motown music. They played Motown hits from the 1960s in the garage, and sports outside. Junior especially loved football, a game he began playing in grade school. His mother hated the idea of him playing a rough contact sport, so she asked him to quit. He refused, telling her he loved it too much.

David and Savaii were very good at sports, but their younger brother was even better. From the start, it was obvious Junior was gifted. He was extremely well coordinated, strong, and fast. He was always tall for his age and fiercely competitive. No matter what sport he was playing, he was always determined to win.

Junior wanted to play Little League baseball, Pop Warner football, and youth league basketball.

Even while signing autographs, Junior manages to remind people of his winning attitude.

His parents, however, could seldom spare the money for fees. So Junior played primarily on after-school sports teams and at the local Boys Club. No matter which sport or which league, Junior's team usually came out on top.

"He was a gifted athlete all the way through elementary school," said Pat Kimbrel, then football coach at Oceanside High School. Now the school's athletic director, Kimbrel has followed Junior's athletic career from the start. Like other coaches at the high school, Kimbrel was eager for Junior to enter ninth grade. He knew the Jefferson Junior High School athlete of the year would make a smooth transition to high school competition.

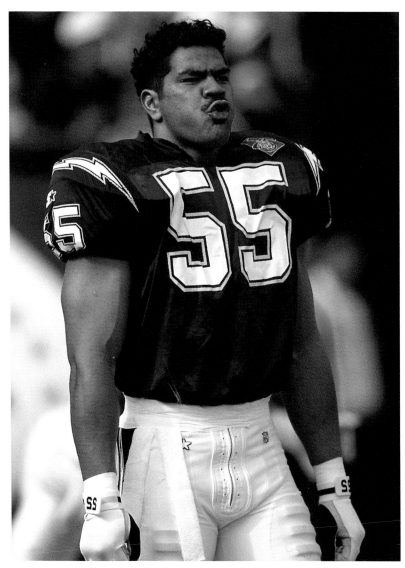

Playing for the Chargers has brought Junior national fame, but he has been successful at all levels of competition.

High School Sensation

3

Junior was 14 when he began ninth grade at Oceanside High School in the fall of 1983. He was big: 6 feet tall and nearly 200 pounds. He earned a starting position as defensive end for the junior varsity football squad and was the team's backup quarterback. He also played linebacker at times.

Even as a freshman, Junior was a superb athlete, said Pat Kimbrel. His older brothers had starred on Oceanside High School's sports teams, but their impact was nothing like Junior's.

Junior's father realized his third son was unusually gifted. Throughout Junior's childhood, the Seaus struggled to make ends meet while raising six children. Tiaina required the children to get after-school jobs to help the family financially. But he made an exception for Junior and allowed his namesake to concentrate on high school sports.

Junior knew his family was making a sacrifice for him, and he was determined to excel and make them proud of him. "The opportunity I was given was special in my family," Junior told the *San Jose Mercury News*. "It's not a debt or something I feel I have to pay back. It's something you respect."

In addition to football, Junior played basketball, baseball, and threw discus and shot put on the track team during his freshman year.

"He was always an intense competitor, and intense on the playing field," said Kimbrel, who coached Junior during his first three seasons of high school football. "Sometimes it could hurt him. Occasionally we had to remind him that he needed to loosen up and enjoy playing more."

Junior's teammates looked up to him because of his athletic ability, work habits, and fiercely competitive attitude during games. "He was a real aggressive, take-charge kind of guy," Kimbrel recalls. "He's always been a gamer. When it came time to play, nobody was more fierce than he was."

No matter what sport he was playing, Junior had a single goal in mind—winning. He hated losing, particularly because he hated disappointing his father. Tiaina would ignore Junior after a loss, and Junior didn't like getting the silent treatment. "If we lost, Dad would act like we were failures," Savaii told *Sports Illustrated*. "He'd say, 'You're lazy.'"

Preparation has been a key to Junior's success as a pro football player.

Winning his father's approval motivated Junior to work hard. Most mornings through high school, he woke up early. He would lift dumbbells in the garage while his brothers slept. Most evenings, he would do hundreds of sit-ups and push-ups in the garage. Then he'd go into the backyard and do dozens of chin-ups from the limb of a maple tree.

"He was always interested in preparing himself," Kimbrel said. "He loved the weight room."

Junior played on the varsity football, basketball, and baseball teams during his sophomore year. In his junior year, he played wide receiver and middle linebacker for Oceanside, whose teams were nicknamed the Pirates.

Junior's emotions got away from him during a basketball game his junior year. Game officials ejected him from a game against rival El Camino High School for fighting, and he was suspended for the next game. Junior hated missing an opportunity to compete. Embarrassed by his behavior, he learned a valuable lesson about how important it is to maintain control during a game.

"He struggled with his emotions, and went through a maturation process like any other adolescent," Coach Kimbrel said.

As a senior in 1986, Junior was one of the top two-way prep football players in the country. He had 123 tackles and five interceptions as an outside linebacker. As a tight end, he caught 71 passes and scored 15 touchdowns. His contributions led the Pirates to a city championship.

Junior's family, including numerous aunts, uncles, and cousins, attended Oceanside High School's football games to cheer for him. Everyone chipped in money to reward Junior for outstanding plays. "For an interception they gave him $10, and for a sack $10," Bill Christopher, one of his high school coaches, told the *New York Times*. "One day, they paid up and he had a wad of bills that could choke a horse."

Honors came flooding in after the season ended. Junior won the defensive MVP award for San Diego County and the offensive MVP award for the Avocado

League, in which his school competed. He received national recognition when he was named to *Parade Magazine*'s All-America football team.

Junior's final high school basketball and track seasons were also memorable. He led the Pirates' basketball team to the league championship during the winter. In the spring, he was the league's top shot putter.

Academically, Junior also excelled. After earning mediocre grades as a freshman, he got serious about his studies. By taking his schoolwork seriously, Junior earned straight A's in his sophomore, junior, and senior years. He graduated from Oceanside High School in June 1987 with a 3.6 grade-point average.

Junior always has worked hard to fight through the offensive line.

4

Trojan Workhorse

Recruiters from more than a dozen colleges offered Junior scholarships to play football at their schools. He considered the offers carefully and narrowed them down to two colleges. He liked Colorado State, where several of his friends had gone. He was also interested in the University of Southern California at Los Angeles, about 60 miles from home. Eventually, he chose USC so his family could watch him play in home games.

Before he even arrived on campus, Junior had a stunning setback. The score from his SAT—a college entrance exam—was too low for him to play football during his first year at USC. Junior had done well on the math portion of the test, but he had problems with the verbal part. Together, the test scores totaled 690—10 points lower than the NCAA required for freshman athletes.

Junior was extremely disappointed and felt he'd let himself and his family down. He also worried that his low SAT scores made his high school look inadequate.

"Everything I'd worked for, everything my family had stood for was gone," Junior told *Sports Illustrated.* "I was labeled a dumb jock."

In the fall, Junior made a visit to Oceanside High School to apologize to his teachers and coaches for letting them down. "He's an emotional type of guy and he was very passionate about it," Kimbrel said. "He also came back to the school again during spring [football practice] to talk to the kids about the importance of grades."

Junior made the most of his setback. Since he couldn't compete on the football field, he concentrated on his classroom studies. Junior also spent hours in the USC weight room. If he wasn't in class, studying, or lifting weights, friends were almost sure to find Junior watching videotapes of football games.

"That first year really whetted his appetite for football," said Larry Smith, Junior's head football coach at USC. "He couldn't play the game he dearly loved, so he'd study tapes and films, particularly offenses. He really developed some good habits and great football instincts during the layoff."

In his sophomore season, Junior saw a lot of action as a backup—primarily in pass rushing situations. Led by quarterback Rodney Peete, the Trojans won their first 10 games and finished the 1988 season at 10-1. They were 8-0 in Pac-10 conference games and earned a trip to the Rose Bowl against the University of Michigan. USC led 14-3 at halftime, but couldn't stop a Wolverine rally in the second half. Michigan won, 22-14.

Junior was ready and eager to play in the fall of 1989. On the first day of football practice, the Trojans were running a pass-rush drill. Junior took a swipe at the ball and got his finger caught on the helmet of another player. He sustained a nasty, painful injury. His finger was broken and nearly torn off his hand.

Even after sustaining a serious finger injury, Junior played with enthusiasm.

Doctors closed the wound and set Junior's hand in a cast. Still, his finger was so sensitive that every time Junior moved his hand, waves of pain shot up his arm.

"He didn't miss a beat," Smith said. "He was back at practice two days later. He also hurt an ankle that same fall, but he kept coming back."

Despite the injuries, Junior earned a spot as the team's starting outside linebacker. "He was a fantastic athlete; very strong, quick, talented, and very intense on the football field," Smith said. "We could have played him at any position and he would have excelled, but he loved playing linebacker."

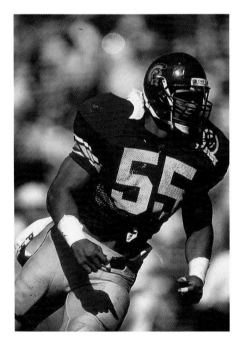

Junior saw action as a backup during his sophomore year, mostly in pass-rushing situations.

USC coach
Larry Smith

USC lost its season opener to Illinois, which squeaked past the Trojans, 14-13. Two weeks later, the Trojans punished Utah State, 66-10, at the Los Angeles Coliseum. Junior sacked Utah's quarterback three times, while USC's freshman quarterback, Todd Marinovich, guided the offense. The following week, Junior had an even bigger game against Ohio State. He deflected four passes, pressured Ohio State's quarterback four times and sacked him twice. USC's defense held Ohio State to a single field goal, while its offense scored six touchdowns for a 42-3 victory.

31

Teammates, fans, and opponents began to take notice. On the field, Junior was intense, focused, and inspired. Off the field, he was modest and polite. "He's a class individual," Smith said. "I can't say enough about him."

USC rattled off three more victories before falling to Notre Dame, 28-24, in late October. The following week, Junior had seven tackles and three sacks as the Trojans shut out Stanford, 19-0. His performance netted him Pac-10 Defensive Player of the Week honors. He had an even stronger game a week later. Against Oregon State, Junior had four sacks to break a USC record of 13 in a season. He made 7 tackles, tying a Trojan season mark of 18. He also recovered a fumble in USC's 48-6 victory.

USC beat Arizona 24-3 in its next-to-last regular-season game and earned a third straight trip to the Rose Bowl. The following week, Junior separated his shoulder in a sloppy 10-10 tie with UCLA. Before the injury forced him from the game, Junior made 3 tackles to finish the regular season with 25 tackles.

On January 1, the Trojans faced the University of Michigan in a Rose Bowl rematch. The Trojans got on the scoreboard first, after a USC player blocked a Michigan punt. Junior picked up the ball and ran it to the Wolverines' 11-yard line. Six plays later, USC quarterback Todd Marinovich scored on a 1-yard run. USC went on to win the game, 17-10.

Junior gets a jump on his opponent during a 1989 game.

Junior's teammates voted him USC's Most Valuable Player for the 1989 season. *The Sporting News* magazine, Associated Press, *College and Pro Football Newsweekly* and UPI all named him to their All-America teams. Both the Pac-10 and USC gave him Defensive Player of the Year awards.

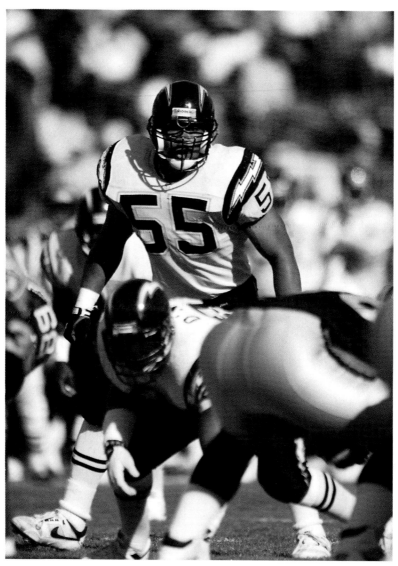

Junior showcased his talent as a young pro with the
Chargers.

5

Charging to Greatness

After the 1989 football season ended, Junior had to make a big decision. Pro football teams were preparing for the spring 1990 draft. If Junior planned to leave college a year early and begin a professional career, he needed to inform the National Football League. As one of the nation's top college football players in 1989, Junior was forecast as a first-round draft selection.

Junior had dreamed about playing in the NFL since grade school. But getting an education was also important to him—and to his parents. Junior had worked hard in his college classes and was well on his way to a degree in public administration. While he was considering his options, Junior asked Coach Smith for advice. "I told him if you are going to leave school early, do it [only] for a first-round pick," Smith recalled.

After discussing it with his parents, Junior decided to turn pro. "With guaranteed money he had an opportunity that was hard to turn down," Coach Smith said.

The San Diego Chargers selected Junior with the fifth pick of the entire draft. Junior used his first NFL paycheck to buy his parents a new house and a new car. He urged his father, who was working as a school custodian, to retire, but Tiaina Sr. refused.

The Charger coaches wanted their rookie to play inside linebacker. Junior, who had focused on pass rushing in college, set about learning his new role.

"At Southern Cal all I did was rush the passer or chase the ball," Junior told *Sports Illustrated*. "Now, for the first time, I've got an awareness of the [defensive] scheme, so I can attack with more intensity."

Intensity was one thing the coaches didn't need to teach Junior. During his first professional game—a preseason contest against the Raiders—Junior showed his fierce competitiveness. Less than a minute into the game, officials ejected Junior for fighting with a Raider player.

The Chargers flew to Dallas to face the Cowboys in their 1990 season opener. Junior didn't start the game, but he played well as a backup. Although Dallas won the game, 17-14, San Diego's coaches were impressed by Junior's efforts. They named him the starting inside linebacker.

As a rookie, Junior quickly learned his new position at in-side linebacker for the Charger defense. He started 15 of the 16 games San Diego played in 1990.

Junior was upset by his teammates' attitude after the first game. He didn't think they were disturbed about losing. "Everybody got on the plane and started gambling," he told the *New York Times*. "It didn't feel as if someone was hurt. I was hurt. I take football seriously."

As the season progressed, Junior realized he could not rely solely on his athletic ability to shine in the NFL. Although he could bench-press 500 pounds and run 40 yards in 4.61 seconds, Junior knew he had a lot to learn about the professional game.

Junior practices hard so he won't have to turn up the intensity at game time. "When I get on the field on Sunday, it should be easy," he says.

Junior responds to the offense's play.

He turned to Gary Plummer, the Chargers' veteran linebacker, for help. Together they studied game films and analyzed offensive plays. Plummer was impressed by how hard Junior worked during their study sessions, team practices, and in the weight room.

"You don't very often see a player with his ability also have his work ethic," Plummer told the *San Jose Mercury News*. "It's a rare combination that somebody like Jerry Rice has."

Plummer was also amazed by how quickly Junior's on-field play improved once he began studying offenses. "You can see the elevated play, how much better he's become by not just relying on ability," Plummer said.

The Chargers won just six games in 1990, finishing fourth in the AFC West. Junior's best performance came in the season finale against the Raiders. He had 12 tackles and his first NFL sack in a 17-12 loss. For the season, Junior had 85 tackles—second best among the Chargers that year.

Junior blossomed into the Chargers' top defensive player during his second season, in 1991. San Diego adopted a defensive game plan in which Junior alternated between inside and outside linebacker. No matter where he lined up, Junior always seemed to know where the ball was headed after the snap. In late September, he had 10 tackles at Denver's Mile High Stadium during a 27-19 loss. Three weeks later, he made a season-high 13 tackles against the Los Angeles Rams. The Chargers' top tackler in 9 of the 16 games he started that year, Junior finished the season with a team-high 129 tackles. He also recorded seven sacks—second best on the squad—and was invited to play in the postseason Pro Bowl. But the Chargers faltered. The team finished with a 4-12 record. Junior, who had grown accustomed to playing in the postseason during college, was disappointed.

USC had lost only three games during his entire time there, Junior told the *New York Times,* and the Trojans had played in three Rose Bowls. Playing in the postseason seemed natural.

During the off-season, Junior kept busy. Along with his wife, Gina, he started the Junior Seau Foundation to help youngsters in the San Diego area. It was his way of doing something to benefit the community, which had offered him so much support throughout his amateur and professional career.

In 1991 Junior emerged as a real force and had his first Pro-Bowl season.

The foundation supports efforts to prevent child abuse, chemical dependency, and juvenile delinquency. The foundation's "TEAM Seau" program offers a "Junior Membership" to encourage kids to be good citizens by staying free of drugs and gangs.

"My hope is for this foundation to help kids face their life challenges with hope and dignity," Junior said. "I see myself in these kids, and if I can be important to the youth of San Diego, then I've accomplished something."

Working with a partner, Bobby Grillo, Junior also started a business selling the colorful shorts, T-shirts, visors, and flip-flop sandals he enjoys wearing. The company is called "Say Ow Gear," and its product line has become popular with teenagers and young adults.

Because he likes the clothing so much, Junior often is a walking billboard for Say-Ow Gear.

Before the 1992 season began, the Chargers hired a new head coach, Bobby Ross. After losing four straight, the Chargers turned things around. San Diego won 11 of its last 12 games and finished first in the AFC West. Once again, Junior was the team's top tackler, this time with 102. He also had 4½ sacks and two interceptions. His teammates and coaches called him the "heart and soul" of the Charger defense.

"He's the best linebacker that ever played the game," Gary Plummer told the *New York Times* in January 1993. "He plays inside, outside, the pass rush. He smothers receivers, stuffs backs. The guy is flying all over the field and making things happen."

San Diego shut out Kansas City, 17-0, in the Chargers' first playoff game since 1982. A week later, the Miami Dolphins beat the Chargers, 31-0, in the AFC divisional playoff game. Before heading off to play in his second Pro Bowl Game, Junior spent $14,000 on a full-page advertisement in the *San Diego Union-Tribune.* The ad, which ran on Super Bowl Sunday, included numerous photos of Charger fans. The copy read: "TO THE FANS OF SAN DIEGO. I THANK YOU FOR A WONDERFUL YEAR. JUNIOR SEAU AND FAMILY."

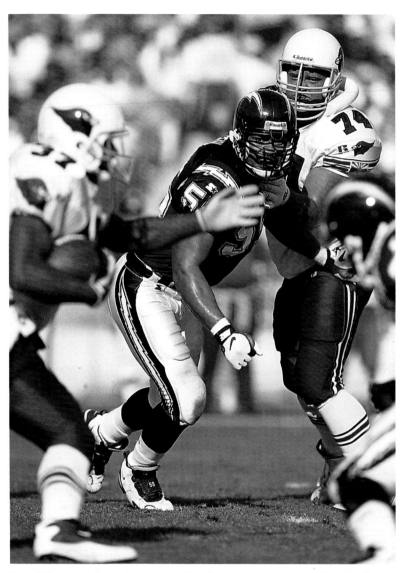

Brushing aside a blocker, Junior moves in on the ballcar-
rier during a game with the Arizona Cardinals.

Impact Player

Junior Seau was looking forward to the start of the 1993 football season. After being the AFC West champs in 1992, the Chargers were hoping to get to the Super Bowl in 1993. Junior had another reason to be excited. Gina was pregnant with their first child. The baby was due in late October, and Junior was looking forward to becoming a father. Just before the season started, however, Gina went into labor, two months early. The Seaus' daughter, Sydney Beau, was very weak and spent her first few weeks in the hospital. Junior and Gina were gravely worried. "Her lungs weren't developed," Junior told *Sport.* "We almost lost her."

Then, soon after Sydney was strong enough to go home with her parents, the family was rocked with another crisis. Junior's youngest brother, Tony, then 15, had joined a gang.

"The influences of the 'hood are powerful, even for a soft-hearted kid like Tony," Junior said. "He got caught up in the wrong crowd."

One night, Tony's gang got into a brawl with another gang. Tony brought a baseball bat to the fight. Several people were badly injured in the battle. Tony was arrested for assault, convicted, and sent to prison. Junior, who spends hours of his free time trying to keep youngsters out of trouble, was heartbroken. He hadn't been able to convince his brother that violence is wrong.

"I preach to Tony what I've preached to all groups I've spoken to," Junior told *Sport*. "We can go out and try to guide them, try to set an example, but we can't make their choices. They must. And they must live with those choices."

Despite all the turmoil he was facing off the field, Junior left his personal problems on the sidelines at game time. He made seven tackles in a game against the Houston Oilers, deflected two passes, and intercepted two more. Both interceptions led to Charger touchdowns and helped lead San Diego to an 18-17 victory. In a game against the Minnesota Vikings, Junior teamed up with defensive end Leslie O'Neal to set up a Charger touchdown. O'Neal started the action by recovering a Viking fumble. After advancing the ball 13 yards, he lateraled it to Junior, who gained an additional 13 yards.

Junior runs back an interception during a 1993 game with the Houston Oilers.

Three weeks later, Junior teamed with O'Neal again on a similar play. This time, it was Junior who forced the Indianapolis Colts to fumble. He scooped up the ball and lateraled it to O'Neal, who ran for eight yards to set up a San Diego touchdown.

Junior finished the season with 129 tackles, another Pro Bowl invitation, and designation to six different All-Pro teams. His teammates voted him and Leslie O'Neal as the Chargers' Most Valuable Players, and the NFL Players Association named him linebacker of the year. Still, Junior was upset by how the season had gone. San Diego finished fourth in the AFC West with a dismal 8-8 record.

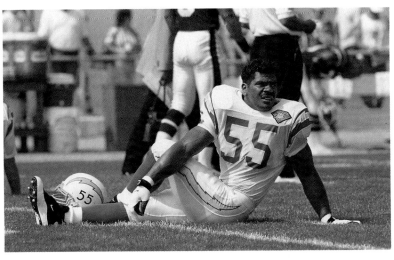

Junior stretches before a game. He's wearing a Chargers' "throw-back" uniform that was part of an NFL anniversary celebration.

"Disappointing is too mild a word," Junior said. "I can sit here and make a number of excuses, including injuries. But the fact is we just weren't good enough to reach the level we did in '92."

The Chargers started the 1994 season with a come-from-behind victory against the Denver Broncos. Junior, who made 14 tackles, stopped a Bronco scoring drive late in the fourth quarter. When the ball slipped out of quarterback John Elway's hands, Junior smothered it. The recovery gave San Diego possession during the waning seconds of the game to preserve a 37-34 lead. Junior was making big plays and disrupting offenses every game. Quarterbacks throughout the league took note.

"There's not another linebacker who does the things he does," quarterback Warren Moon told *The Sporting News*. "What really sets him apart is he plays with so much enthusiasm and emotion. That helps him get to the ball a little faster."

The Chargers won their first six games before falling to the Broncos, 20-15, in a rematch of their season opener. Even then Junior made the Denver players work hard for the victory. He sacked Elway once and made a career-high 19 tackles.

In late November, Junior was injured in a 23-17 loss against the New England Patriots. After making 11 tackles, he pinched a nerve in his neck. The injury was painful, but Junior refused to miss any games.

The Chargers, who dropped to 8-3 with the loss, were shooting for the playoffs. Junior was determined to help them reach that goal.

He helped San Diego clinch the AFC West title with 11 tackles in the final game of the season—against the New York Jets. The Jets took an early lead on a field goal and were driving toward the end zone in the second quarter when Junior tackled quarterback Boomer Esiason. Esiason left the game with a concussion, and the momentum shifted from the Jets to the Chargers, who won 21-6. "That was a big thing for us because Boomer is the leader of their offense," Junior said. "We got it going after that."

With some help from his teammates, Junior (far right) brings down Indianapolis Colt Lamar Warren.

With Junior in hot pursuit, Jerry Rice hauls in a pass during the Super Bowl.

The Chargers carried the momentum into the post-season. After defeating Miami, 22-21, in the first round of the playoffs, they upset the Pittsburgh Steelers to reach the Super Bowl. The AFC champs, however, were no match for the San Francisco 49ers in Super Bowl XXIX. Guided by quarterback Steve Young, the 49ers became Super Bowl champions with a 49-26 win.

Once again, Junior was the Chargers' leading tackler with 155 in the regular season and 31 in the post-season. He was again invited to the Pro Bowl and named linebacker of the year by the NFL Players Association. Because of Junior's game performances and his community service work, he was named the NFL's Man of the Year for 1994.

Junior, with Gina and Sydney, enjoys some free time during the week of the 1995 Pro Bowl in Hawaii.

Junior's family grew in 1995, when Gina gave birth to a healthy baby boy shortly after the season began. The Seaus named their second child Jake Ryan. Junior was happy off the field, but not so happy about the way San Diego was playing. The Chargers got off to a dismal start, losing the season opener to the Oakland Raiders. Although the Chargers' defense was strong, the offense stumbled during the first half of the season. San Diego fell to the bottom of the AFC West standings in mid-November, then bounced back with a five-game winning streak. The strong finish moved the Chargers into second place in the AFC

West, and earned them a wildcard berth in the play-offs. This time, San Diego lost in the first round, 35-20, to the Indianapolis Colts.

Junior's old high school had a much better season. The Pirates were the top team in their division in 1995, and Junior followed their games with interest. He attended the Pirates' season opener, leaving at halftime when the crush of autograph seekers became too great. The pro linebacker also offered the Pirates moral support during their championship contest.

"He talked to our kids before the title game," said Pat Kimbrel, Oceanside High School's athletic director. "At halftime he stuck his head in the locker room, and [he] congratulated them after the game."

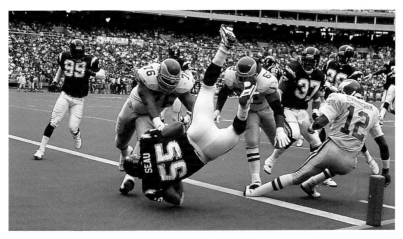

Junior's first NFL touchdown came against Philadelphia during the 1995 season. He recovered a fumble and ran it 29 yards for the score.

Those who know Junior weren't surprised that he'd take time away from his busy schedule to encourage younger athletes. "He's a guy who is very involved in his community and in community service," said Larry Smith, Junior's coach at USC. "He's always doing something off the field for others. He's a real hero."

JUNIOR SEAU'S
FOOTBALL STATISTICS

University of Southern California Trojans

Year	Games	Tackles	Tackles for Lost Yardage	Sacks	Fumbles Recovered	Interceptions	Deflected Passes
1988	10	35	6 (–40)	6	2	0	2
1989	11	72	27 (–148)	19	2	1	12
Totals	**21**	**107**	**33 (–188)**	**25**	**4**	**1**	**14**

College Highlights:

USC Defensive Player of the Year, 1989.
USC Most Valuable Player, 1989.
All-America, 1989.
Pac-10 Defensive Player of the Year, 1989.
All-Pac-10 first team, 1989.

San Diego Chargers—Regular Season

Year	Games	Solo Tackles	Assisted Tackles	Total Tackles	Sacks	Fumbles Forced	Fumbles Recovered	Interceptions
1990	16	61	24	85	1	0	0	0
1991	16	111	18	129	7	0	0	0
1992	15	79	23	102	4½	1	1	2
1993	16	108	21	129	0	1	1	2
1994	16	124	31	155	5½	1	3	0
1995	16	111	18	129	2	1	3	2
Totals	**95**	**594**	**135**	**729**	**20**	**4**	**8**	**6**

Career Highlights:

All-NFL, 1992, 1993, 1994, 1995.
Pro Bowl, 1991, 1992, 1993, 1994, 1995.
NFL Man of the Year, 1994.
Chargers' co-Most Valuable Player, 1993.
NFL Players Association Linebacker of the Year, 1993, 1994.

Index

ACKNOWLEDGMENTS

Photographs are reproduced by permission of: Jamie Squire/Allsport, p. 1; Sports-Chrome East/West/Rich Kane, pp. 2, 38, 44; Simon Bruty/Allsport, p. 6; Archive/Reuters/Ray Stubblebine, p. 10; Paul J. Redfield/North County Times, p. 12; Ted Streshinsky/Photo 20-20, p. 15; Thom Vollenweider/San Diego Chargers, pp. 18, 23, 52; SportsChrome East/West/Louis A. Raynor, p. 20; Stephen Dunn/Allsport, pp. 26, 29, 33, 37, 39, 47, 50; University of Southern California, pp. 30, 31; Sports-Chrome East/West/Rob Tringali Jr., pp. 34, 48; Otto Greule/Allsport, p. 41; Craig Jones/Allsport, p. 42; © Mickey Pfleger, p. 51; and Doug Pensinger/Allsport, p. 53.

Front cover photograph reproduced by permission of Al Bello/Allsport. Back cover photograph reproduced by permission of SportsChrome East/West/Rich Kane.